6/96

D0461426

STREET SMART!

Cities of the Ancient World

STREET SMART!

Cities of the Ancient World

Prepared by Geography Department

Runestone Press ◆ Minneapolis

ᚱᚢᚾᛖᛋᛏᚮᚾᛖ ᛈᚱᛖᛋᛋ • ᚱᚢᚿᚼᛏᛇᛏ

rune (r$\overline{oo}$n) *n* **1 a :** one of the earliest written alphabets used in northern Europe, dating back to A.D. 200; **b :** an alphabet character believed to have magic powers; **c :** a charm; **d :** an Old Norse or Finnish poem. **2 :** a poem or incantation of mysterious significance, often carved in stone.

Street Smart! Cities of the Ancient World is a fully revised and updated edition of *City Planning in Ancient Times,* a title previously published by Lerner Publications Company. The text is completely reset in 12/15 Albertus, and new photographs and captions have been added.

Thanks to Dr. Guy Gibbon, Department of Anthropology, University of Minnesota, for his help in preparing this book.

Words in **bold** type are listed in a glossary that starts on page 77.

Library of Congress Cataloging–in–Publication Data
   Street Smart!: cities of the ancient world / prepared by Geography Department, Runestone Press.
      p. cm—(Buried Worlds)
   Includes index.
   ISBN 0–8225–3208–5 (lib. bdg.)
   1. Cities and towns, Ancient—Juvenile literature. [1. Cities and towns, Ancient.] I. Runestone Press. Geography Dept. II. Series.
HT114.S86 1994
307.76′093—dc20   93–632
                                                                                 CIP
                                                                                 AC

Manufactured in the United States of America
1 2 3 4 5 6 – I/JR – 99 98 97 96 95 94

CONTENTS

THE STUDY OF ANCIENT CITIES

In the modern world, people choose to live in cities for many reasons. Some people are drawn to urban areas by job opportunities. Others come for cultural and recreational activities, such as concerts and sports events. Many residents simply like the rapid pace of city life.

These same qualities appealed to city dwellers in ancient times. While most early people were farmers who lived in rural areas, residents of cities held specialized jobs. Athletic matches, religious ceremonies, and other events drew large numbers of people to urban areas, and marketplaces bustled with activity.

The word *city* comes from the Latin *civitas,* which refers to a community that administers its own affairs. But many **archaeologists** (scientists who dig up and study ancient objects) do not consider early communities to be cities unless they possessed certain other qualities. These requirements include a large population numbering at least several thousand people. Another necessity for a settlement to be a city was that it must have control of an area beyond the city limits. These surrounding lands usually produced enough food for all people in the community so that some city dwellers could then work at nonrural, specialized jobs. In this way, cities acquired a surplus of food and made goods that could be traded to increase the community's wealth.

A team of archaeologists (scientists who dig up and study ancient objects) examines the ruins of an ancient city in the Middle Eastern country of Israel. These experts carefully excavate (dig up) remains layer by layer, sometimes using tools as small as a toothbrush.

The Evolution of Cities

Like modern cities, ancient cities were unique and evolved for a variety of reasons. In prehistoric times, people moved from place to place to hunt and gather food. These hunters, who probably lived in groups of 25 to 50 people, set up temporary camps near water. Members of these nomadic communities performed different jobs in the camps. Some made stone tools and weapons, while others hunted, butchered the kill, or dried fish.

About 8000 B.C., people learned that the plants they gathered for food grew from seeds. These early farmers collected and planted the seeds and began to produce a steady supply of crops for their families. The reliable food source gave people a reason to build permanent villages near their farmland. Ancient farmers invented tools that made their jobs easier and eventually people were able to harvest enough crops to nourish the entire population of a village.

In communities where food supplies were plentiful, some villagers stopped farming and learned other skills, such as pottery making or metalworking. Some villagers became merchants who bought and sold the works of craftspeople.

After prehistoric wanderers learned to plant seeds and to harvest crops, they began to settle in small villages and to farm the surrounding land. The earliest crops included wheat, barley, beans, and squash.

Workers drill and polish beads in this painting, which adorned the wall of an ancient tomb found in the North African country of Egypt. As early villages evolved into cities, many ancient people turned from farming to nonrural pursuits, such as manufacturing and trade.

Other people labored as traders, transporting goods to communities in distant lands. This economic expansion attracted more settlers to the villages. As their populations grew, many villages became towns, and, by 3500 B.C., some of these towns had evolved into cities.

Not all of the world's early cities developed for economic reasons, however. Urban areas often arose near military outposts, most of which were surrounded by tall, defensive walls. Many ancient cities were established for religious purposes. Large communities settled around shrines that religious followers built to honor their gods. Sometimes geographical location fostered the development of a city. Port cities, for instance, often grew near sheltered harbors along busy trade routes.

Many of the world's modern cities began as villages. London, England, for example, was established in the first century A.D. A small seaport, London grew along the banks of the Thames River. As people moved to the village, they built houses wherever they could find unoccupied land and

Some archaeologists believe that the city of Jericho—located between Israel and Jordan in a region called the West Bank—was first inhabited about 8000 B.C. On this site, experts have identified the layered remains of many settlements. Over the centuries, residents of Jericho leveled old buildings and then raised new structures on the same spot.

constructed roads haphazardly. As a result, some of London's winding streets cut across one another at various angles. The routes of these same streets continue to tangle traffic in present-day London.

Ancient City Planning

Not all ancient cities evolved from small villages. Many were deliberately established by a group of people who decided to live in a particular place. The founders of these cities usually had specific ideas about the purpose of their city and the way it should look. Ancient builders found that if they could plan cities, they could minimize urban problems, such as noise, overcrowding, and inefficient waste disposal. By designing cities with wide streets, lush parks, sewer systems, and places for public entertainment, planners could make city life very pleasant.

Ancient architects considered several factors when designing a city. They examined the natural features of the surrounding landscape. Mountains, for example, could slow transportation, and deserts could limit access to water. The city's purpose as a military, religious, economic, or political center was often a key factor in determining its layout. Planners then considered how to divide a city into industrial, commercial, and residential areas.

The design for Washington, D.C.—one of the most famous planned cities in the world—was drawn up by the French architect Pierre Charles L'Enfant in 1791.

DESIGNING THE DISTRICT

In the 1770s, during the American War of Independence, the French architect Pierre Charles L'Enfant volunteered to join the fight against the British. His bravery in battle brought him to the attention of General George Washington.

After becoming president of the United States of America, Washington commissioned the Frenchman in 1791 to plan the new national capital, to be called Washington, District of Columbia. But before beginning his design, L'Enfant carefully considered the purpose of the city and the landscape of the site. He envisioned wide avenues that fanned out from a grand legislative building (now the U.S. Capitol). Broad boulevards would separate the main residential areas, which would be crossed by narrower streets and small public parks.

Although construction of the capital city began under L'Enfant's supervision, the cost of the lavish plan was too high for President Washington's budget. Quarrels between the two men resulted in L'Enfant's dismissal in 1792. Despite the disagreement, however, the layout of modern Washington, D.C., follows L'Enfant's original design.

They plotted the locations of streets and figured out how to transport water and dispose of waste.

Yet ancient cities were not all alike, and design decisions were made in a variety of ways. If the community was ruled by a king, for instance, design choices might be made by just one person. Under a more democratic system, the entire community might have a say in the city's construction.

Another factor affecting the planning of a city was the wealth of its founders. The leaders of great and powerful empires could build magnificent palaces or huge **public works.** But a group of immigrants or retired soldiers might have little money to invest, and the city they planned would probably be modest and simple.

The level of building technology also influenced the look of a city. The Romans, who lived in what is now Italy, knew how to build strong, durable arches that could support structures rising high above the ground. This skill made it possible to construct giant **aqueducts** for carrying water from the distant countryside into the cities.

Archaeology and City Planning

For the last 200 years, archaeologists have been **excavating** (digging up) the remains of civilizations throughout the world. They have

The Pont du Gard, a Roman-built aqueduct, crosses a river near Nîmes, France. Ancient Roman builders constructed this aqueduct with three levels of brick arches that supported a water channel at the top.

This view of the remains of Beersheba (above) in Israel shows the walls and buildings that surrounded the city's main entrance. An excavator (below) removes a large, stone slab from Beersheba's ruins.

found evidence that many ancient cities were planned. Some of the world's oldest urban areas have revealed a clear network of streets and the careful arrangement of parks and public buildings.

The development of aerial photography during the mid-1900s created great interest in ancient city planning. Pictures taken from high above ancient sites revealed faint outlines of walls and foundations that had never been visible from ground level.

These ancient ruins show that city planners were at work thousands of years ago. The art of designing and building a city is not a modern development but rather is one of the oldest professional accomplishments in the world.

ANCIENT CITIES OF THE MIDDLE EAST

More than 5,000 years ago, the world's first civilizations arose in the river valleys of the Middle East, a region where Africa and Asia meet. Farmers in this area channeled river water into ditches and canals to irrigate the land. Because of the Middle East's warm climate, crops grew in abundance. Soon a surplus of food was available to feed the populations of the region's emerging cities.

The Land Between the Rivers

The ancient region of Mesopotamia included what are now eastern Syria, southeastern Turkey, and most of Iraq. Named for the Greek word meaning "between the rivers," Mesopotamia was bound by the Tigris and the Euphrates rivers. Although this region is now mostly desert, it was once covered by swamps and fertile farmland. The earliest city dwellers were the Sumerians, who lived in the Mesopotamian kingdom of Sumer.

The world's first city was probably Uruk in southern Mesopotamia. Arising as early as 4000 B.C., Uruk began as two separate settlements—Kullaba and Eanna. The two communities had joined together to form one large urban area that occupied less than 1 square mile (2.6 square kilometers) and probably housed several thousand people.

14

Two large temple complexes dominated ancient Uruk. Dedicated to the Sumerian sun god Anu, the White Temple stood in the area of the Kullaba settlement. The Limestone and Pillar Temples of Eanna honored Inanna, the goddess of love.

In one of these temples, archaeologists found clay tablets imprinted with symbols called **pictographs.** Scholars believe that the tablets

Ancient artists decorated this clay wall with red, black, and white pegs. The structure, which stands in the Mesopotamian city of Uruk, dates to about 3000 B.C.

helped the Sumerians to keep track of day-to-day inventories and activities, such as the supply and distribution of food. These finds also suggest that the temple was used not only for religious ceremonies but also for administrative and economic purposes.

Because the land in Mesopotamia lacked large deposits of stone, Sumerians collected clay from the riverbanks to mold into building bricks. Artisans also made cone-shaped pegs from clay. After painting them red, black, or white, artists pressed the pegs into the clay walls of temples for decoration.

Archaeologists estimate that by 2500 B.C., with a population of about 50,000, Uruk had grown to almost six times its original size. At this time, the Sumerian king Gilga-

Sumerian scribes used a piece of metal or wood to press wedge-shaped marks into wet clay. This system of writing—the first in the world—is called cuneiform. Priests used cuneiform to track the economic activities of Sumerian cities.

Stepped towers called ziggurats served as the religious, economic, and administrative centers of Sumerian cities.

mesh ordered the construction of a thick protective wall around the city. By 2000 B.C., the Sumerians had built a **ziggurat,** or stepped tower, near the temples of Eanna. Resembling a mountain, the ziggurat held shrines to Sumerian gods.

Most of Uruk remains unexcavated and is still covered by desert sands. For this reason, archaeologists know very little about the city's residential housing or street plans. But the large-scale construction of the temples and city walls indicate that the Sumerians probably engaged in some sort of central planning.

Babylon

Until about 2000 B.C., Babylon was a small Mesopotamian town on the Euphrates River. At that time, invaders from the south seized Babylon and the surrounding region to create the kingdom of Babylonia. Babylon became the capital of this new realm. Throughout the centuries, the city was conquered by several different groups. In 626 B.C., the Babylonians won back their lands, and from 605 to 562 B.C., under King Nebuchadnezzar, they rebuilt Babylon on a grand scale.

Workers constructed an enormous **rampart** (protective barrier) around Babylon. The rampart consisted of two walls set about 40 feet (12 meters) apart. The inside wall was considerably taller than the outside wall. Covered with gravel, the ground between the walls served as a roadway for troops defending the city from attack. For additional protection, laborers dug a wide, water-filled ditch called a **moat** outside the rampart. To enter Babylon, residents and visitors had to cross bridges over the moat and then pass through one of the city's eight bronze gates.

The largest entryway was the magnificent Ishtar Gate, which was named after the principal goddess

Ziggurats dominated ancient Babylon's landscape (above). These important temples reveal Babylon's status as the religious center of Babylonia. Detailed figures of lions (left) adorned the brick walls leading to the Ishtar Gate, the main entrance to Babylon.

of Babylonia. This gate really consisted of two gateways because the city's rampart had two walls. The short outer gate and the tall inner gate each stood between two lookout towers. The entire entrance was covered with shining blue glaze and painted with figures of bulls and dragons. The Ishtar Gate straddled a paved avenue called Processional Way. High walls, elaborately decorated with the images of lions, bordered this road as it led to the entrance.

Inside the rampart, Babylon was shaped like a rectangle. The Euphrates River divided the city into two parts of unequal size connected by a stone bridge. A massive ziggurat made up of seven terraces dominated Babylon's landscape. At the top of this temple, known as the Tower of Babel, stood the Holy of Holies, a gold-roofed shrine dedicated to the Babylonian god Marduk. Within the walled *timenos,* or temple area, were courts, smaller temples, priests' living quarters, and storehouses for offerings made to Marduk.

From excavations, archaeologists have learned about the private homes of the ancient Babylonians. A typical house was built around a central courtyard. For privacy, the dwelling's windows were placed on

The crumbling ruins of Nebuchadnezzar's Royal Palace give archaeologists clues about how the Babylonian king lived and ruled.

interior walls that faced toward the courtyard rather than the street. Floors were made of brick, and walls were whitewashed. Builders fashioned roofs from palm wood overlaid with reed matting. The outside of the house was then covered with a thick layer of mud.

Overlooking the courtyard, the kitchen contained a large cooking hearth made up of two brick platforms. The bottom platform supported the materials for a fire, while the top platform held pots used for cooking. Drainpipes sent wastes from the kitchen to the street. Each household also dedicated a room as a religious shrine to one or more Babylonian gods. Beneath the shrine, a deep, brick-lined shaft held the remains of deceased family members.

The king of Babylonia lived in the elaborate Royal Palace, which had five courtyards. The extensive grounds of the Royal Palace

Stretching along the banks of the Euphrates River, Babylon was an important regional trading center.

Lush, green fields bordering the Nile River meet the desert sands that cover most of Egypt. The ancient Egyptians, who built their cities in the Nile River Valley, depended on the waterway for irrigation and transportation.

included the Hanging Gardens of Babylon, built by King Nebuchadnezzar. The garden, which stood 75 feet (23 m) tall, was made up of a series of terraces covered with layers of soil deep enough to support large trees. Shrubs, ferns, and trailing plants also grew on the terraces, which were irrigated by water from the Euphrates.

Egyptian Public Works

In Egypt, a large country in North Africa, most people live on long, narrow strips of land on either side of the Nile River. This inhabited region is surrounded by barren desert. The Nile rises in the mountains of East Africa and runs northward through the Sahara Desert until it empties into the Mediterranean Sea. In July and August, the waters of the Nile overflow the riverbanks and deposit a fertile layer of soil on the plains along the river. For thousands of years, the Egyptians have depended on this annual flooding to grow crops.

To ensure a good harvest, the ancient Egyptians built dams and canals to control the flow of water. In this way, farmers could direct the

Using a mechanical device called a shaduf, *an ancient Egyptian worker draws water from the Nile to fill an irrigation ditch. These artificial channels carried water to distant croplands.*

floodwaters to storage areas for use in irrigation. Most archaeologists and historians believe that the Egyptian kings, called pharaohs, controlled these complicated irrigation and farming projects from cities.

From **hieroglyphics**—a system of picture writing—historians know that the Egyptians had been designing complex public works long before they constructed their first

cities. The layouts of irrigation projects and of huge pyramids—pointed, triangular structures that held the tombs of the pharaohs—showed that Egyptians employed many advanced building techniques.

To raise the pyramids at Giza on the west bank of the Nile, for example, workers first leveled the land. Then they dug a ditch to serve as a reference point for the

Early Egyptians carved pyramid stones (above) *by hand and carefully fit them together without mortar. Modern-day travelers are dwarfed by the imposing walls of an ancient pyramid* (right).

pyramid's boundaries. Crews constructed a road to the riverbank, so that enormous building stones shipped from the north could be easily unloaded onto sleds mounted on greased runners. Thousands of laborers were needed to pull the heavy sleds to the pyramid site and to lift the stones into place.

In this ancient stone carving, Egyptian builders haul heavy construction materials up ladders.

This illustration of Great Zimbabwe shows workers building the city's massive wall.

THE CITY THE SHONA BUILT

In about A.D. 1000, the Shona, a Bantu-speaking people of southern Africa, founded a strong commercial empire that covered most of what is now Zimbabwe. From this location, Shona leaders traded their gold, cloth, ivory, and iron for beads, brass, and other goods. These items were carried by merchants who traveled inland from the coast of the Indian Ocean.

In the Shona language, *zimbabwe* means "houses of stone." The term comes from the stone ruins of a large city, known as Great Zimbabwe, that flourished from the thirteenth to the fifteenth centuries. Archaeologists believe that Great Zimbabwe was one of the earliest international trading hubs in southern Africa.

The builders of Great Zimbabwe took full advantage of the natural resources near the site. Large granite blocks cut from the surrounding hillsides, for example, were used as the material for thick walls and massive towers. Clay for surfacing walls and grass for roofing were also readily available. Three large enclosures in the city housed markets, religious shrines, royal palaces, and the homes of artisans. Great Zimbabwe's impressive structures make it one of the most important archaeological sites in Africa.

A modern drawing shows a large house in Tell al-Amarna, a planned city that was built as the Egyptian capital in the fourteenth century B.C. This enormous villa contained large, open courtyards. The surrounding wall provided privacy.

Tell al-Amarna

The most spectacular planned city of ancient Egypt was Tell al-Amarna, which dates to the fourteenth century B.C. Until that time, the capital of Egypt was the southeastern city of Thebes. Tell al-Amarna, located along the Nile in east central Egypt, was built after a young pharaoh named Akhenaton came to power in 1364 B.C. The pharaohs before him had worshiped many gods and had ruled over societies with vast inequalities between the rich and the poor. Akhenaton dreamed of a kingdom in which all people would be equal and united under a single god.

During his reign, Akhenaton abolished the worship of the old gods and announced that everyone would honor only the sun god, Aton. Akhenaton dedicated Tell al-Amarna, the new capital, to Aton. Workers built the city on the east bank of the Nile, about 250 miles

(400 km) up the river from Thebes. Tell al-Amarna was vast, with wide streets and spacious houses. In keeping with Akhenaton's philosophy of unity and peace, a wall did not surround the city. Instead, stone pillars marked the urban boundaries.

Tell al-Amarna was very different from other ancient cities, both in form and in function. The royal complex stood in the heart of the city and was surrounded by the houses of servants and government officials. The large royal facility consisted of ceremonial palaces, residences for the pharaoh and his family, and a series of temples dedicated to Aton.

The paintings that adorned palace walls also differed from previous Egyptian artworks. For the first time, the pharaoh was portrayed not as a powerful and frightening figure but as an ordinary person. The palace paintings show Akhenaton playing with his children and picking flowers. And, although it was rare for Egyptian artists to depict emotion, the people in these paintings have smiling faces.

A broad avenue led south from the royal complex to another complex that held shrines, pavilions, and artificial lakes. Other streets were arranged haphazardly. Rich and poor people lived together in residential areas, and one section housed only skilled workers, such as stone masons and painters.

Tell al-Amarna did not outlive Akhenaton's reign. His successor moved the royal capital back to Thebes and returned to the old religion that worshiped many gods. Over time, the abandoned city fell into ruin.

A detailed stone carving portrays the pharaoh Akhenaton and his wife Nefertiti making offerings to the sun god Aton. Akhenaton built Tell al-Amarna to honor this important god.

ANCIENT CITIES OF ASIA

Like the early civilizations of Mesopotamia and Egypt, the inhabitants of ancient Asia depended on large river systems to irrigate their land for farming. Small agricultural settlements in the Indus River Valley and in the regions surrounding the Huang (Yellow) River of China gradually evolved into great cities.

Mohenjo-Daro and Harappa

Located along the Indus River in what is now Pakistan and parts of northwestern India, the Indus Valley spread over approximately 386,000 square miles (1 million sq km). The Indus civilization thrived from 2400 to 1650 B.C. A peaceful group, the Indus people were ruled by priest-kings from the twin capitals of Mohenjo-Daro and Harappa.

Mohenjo-Daro, the largest of the Indus cities, was built near the Indus River in what is now southern Pakistan. Archaeologists estimate that the city's population numbered about 35,000 people. Most of the residents were merchants, who traded agricultural goods and crafts for metal, stone, and spices.

From excavations, archaeologists have determined that the city was built according to a specific plan carried out by a large crew of laborers. Standardization of architecture was vital to the city's planners, who designed all sewers, drains,

Built of mud and brick, a fortress dominates the ruins of Mohenjo-Daro (above). *This city was the largest of the Indus civilization, which thrived in the region that is now Pakistan and India. Archaeologists have been studying the Asian settlement since the 1920s and have discovered many artifacts, including animal figures* (right).

houses, and even bricks to conform to a specific pattern.

Encircled by a wall, Mohenjo-Daro was divided into two sections, one of which was reserved for administrative buildings and the other for housing. Located in the western half of the city, the administrative section stood on a mud and brick mound overlooking the residential area to the east. Workers built the residential area according to a grid pattern, with the homes located on a series of rectangular blocks. Streets neatly divided the grid.

Mohenjo-Daro's homes were simple brick dwellings built for comfort. Each house consisted of a central courtyard, which provided air and light, and a surrounding cluster of rooms. Two stories high, the houses had staircases leading to an upper floor and to the roof, where residents often slept on hot summer nights. Because of the region's warm weather, homes had few win-

Excavated from the ruins of Mohenjo-Daro, this stone statue probably depicts one of the city's rulers—a priest-king.

This replica of a seal found at Mohenjo-Daro includes a carving of a bull accompanied by ancient Indus writing symbols, which archaeologists have yet to decipher.

dows or doors, which would have let light and heat into the rooms.

Most houses contained a private well and a bathroom that was hooked up to the city's sewer system. Clay pipes in the bathroom wall allowed waste to run into an underground pool called a cesspit, where sewage was filtered from the water. After the sifting process, the waste drained through a channel under the streets and was carried outside the city. Manholes in the city streets could be opened if a blockage occured in the sewer.

Archaeologists also discovered bathrooms in the administrative section. A building called the Great Bath featured eight private, paved bathrooms, which may have been reserved for priests. The building's main attraction, a large bathing pool surrounded by pillars, may have been used for religious ceremonies. Workers sealed the brick pool with layers of cement and clay to make the structure watertight. A drain beneath the pool's sloping floor allowed dirty water to flow out.

31

The Indus River and its tributaries watered productive farmlands (left) that served early Indus cities. These waterways often changed course, leaving some urban areas without water.

Workshops found at Mohenjo-Daro suggest that the city's residents specialized in industry and commerce. Craftspeople made pots, vases, dishes, and ornaments from copper and bronze. Other artisans created necklaces and earrings from gold or made beads from semiprecious stones. Mohenjo-Daro's traders sold these goods to nearby cities and towns.

About 1750 B.C., Mohenjo-Daro began to decline. Experts speculate that, since few weapons have been found at the site, invaders easily could have killed or driven out Mohenjo-Daro's peaceful population. Other scientists believe that repeated flooding or a change in climate forced people to leave.

Lying 400 miles (640 km) southwest of Mohenjo-Daro, the city of Harappa arose in 2350 B.C. The Indus people built Harappa on the Ravi tributary of the Indus River in central Pakistan. Harappa is known as the Indus "mother city" because it was the first city discovered in the Indus Valley. Little is left of the site, however. Over time, people seeking free building materials took the city's bricks.

Although archaeologists have had trouble analyzing Harappa, they have discovered that the city shared many similarities with Mohenjo-Daro. Like Mohenjo-Daro, Harappa consisted of an administrative area and a residential section, which also included burial grounds. The city's straight streets crossed one another at right angles. Because river flooding on Harappa's flat plain posed continuous problems, workers built structures on raised mud platforms.

Harappa's burial grounds, which remained more intact than other areas of the city, reveal that funeral practices changed gradually over time. At first, residents buried their dead in the ground, probably in wooden coffins. In the graves, archaeologists found bodies positioned north to south, with the heads turned to the west. Funeral pottery—such as bowls, flasks, vases, and water pots—lay nearby.

In later graves, Harappa's citizens placed remains in burial pots. These bodies had probably been hung on trees for birds of prey and other wild animals to eat and then buried at a later date. Over time, the Harappan burial pots became more decorative and finely crafted.

Many Harappans were farmers. Their main crops were peas, wheat, and barley, which the city kept in a large storage facility called a granary. The huge Harappan granary measured 168 feet (51 m) long and 135 feet (41 m) wide and consisted of rows of storage buildings with wooden floors and brick walls. Holes in the end walls of each storehouse allowed air to circulate freely, a condition that kept food dry and helped to prevent rotting. Workers constructed rampways around the storehouses so that carts could drive right into the granary.

Like Mohenjo-Daro, Harappa was eventually abandoned. Experts believe that Harappans, who were strongly dependent on the Ravi for irrigation and travel, left the city when the waterway began to flow away from Harappa.

Excavators at Harappa unearthed pieces of an ancient game.

Zhengzhou and An-yang

In China, far east of the Indus Valley, ancient cities developed along the Huang River. The Huang carried fertile silt southeastward from the highlands of China to its dry northern plains. This rich soil allowed farmers in the region to grow abundant crops of millet, rice, wheat, and barley. From 1700 B.C. to 1100 B.C., the powerful kings of the Shang dynasty (family of rulers) dominated northern China and established the cities of Zhengzhou and An-yang.

Between 1600 B.C. and 1400 B.C., when the Shang dynasty was at its height, Zhengzhou expanded and flourished as a political and military center. Ancient Zhengzhou was located south of the Huang River on the same site as the present-day city.

Covering an area of about 1 square mile (2.6 sq km), Zheng-

Rivers running from China's west central mountains bring water to terraced rice paddies. For thousands of years, rice has been a staple food in the Chinese diet.

zhou was surrounded by a huge, rectangular wall constructed with the *hangtu* (packed earth) technique. Using this method, workers pressed horizontal layers of dirt between vertical wooden supports. Each successive layer was firmly packed before adding another. Zhengzhou's defensive wall measured about 33 feet (10 m) high and 66 feet (20 m) wide. To build a wall this size, 10,000 workers would have toiled almost nonstop for nearly 13 years.

Within the protective wall, the city was divided into a series of rectangular blocks. Wood and thatch houses were built in clusters and had hangtu floors. Archaeologists discovered a similar hangtu floor within a large rectangular structure thought to be a palace or administrative building. A hangtu platform, which was probably an altar, stood nearby.

Outside the city wall, archaeologists found villages containing more houses, as well as workshops

A Shang artisan crafted a jade ceremonial knife (above), which was probably a copy of a real weapon. Shang warriors wore bronze helmets (right) to protect themselves while defending their cities.

Shang craftspeople were famous for their intricately cast bronzeworks. The shape and markings of this vessel suggest that it was used in burial rites.

where craftspeople molded pottery, carved bones, and cast bronze objects. These sites suggest that the inhabitants of Zhengzhou held specialized jobs and produced goods on a large scale.

Located north of Zhengzhou, the city of An-yang prospered during the twelfth century B.C. Scholars believe that An-yang once served as the center of the Shang dynasty's administrative, ceremonial, and manufacturing activities.

Ancient work crews employed many of Zhengzhou's city-planning and architectural techniques in the construction of An-yang. Houses, administrative buildings, ceremonial structures, and workshops featured the hangtu style. Excavators have

been studying the site, which occupies 9 square miles (24 sq km), since 1928. The evidence they have uncovered suggests that An-yang was a city of great power but was subject to frequent invasion. Numerous weapons and chariots (horse-drawn battle carts) have been discovered in An-yang's burial tombs. Archaeologists also unearthed many wooden-handled bronze daggers and heavy bronze axes.

A large burial complex in the city contained a royal cemetery, as well as more than 1,000 other graves. The Shang constructed the royal tombs in a north-to-south, cross-shaped design with ramps leading down to the main burial

THE WORLD'S LONGEST STRUCTURE

Although collapsed in some areas, the Great Wall of China remains the longest structure ever built. The earliest sections date to the fifth century B.C. The Shang dynasty extended the wall in the third century B.C., and later additions lengthened it to nearly 4,000 miles (6,437 kilometers). One continuous segment stretches for 2,150 miles (3,460 km) near the Chinese capital of Beijing.

Built as protection from Mongol invaders, the Great Wall stretches from north central China almost to the northeastern coast. Builders raised the structure to an average height of 25 feet (7.6 meters). In places where stone was plentiful, the stout wall was constructed of granite. At other spots, stone was scarce, so workers molded moistened soil into a solid earthen barrier.

Every 100 to 200 yards (90 to 180 m), workers built a tall watchtower from which soldiers could scan the horizon for invaders. If foreign armies were spotted, Chinese troops massed atop the wall. The structure was wide enough to fit rows of 10 soldiers, who could march shoulder to shoulder along the wall's length.

Tourists stroll along the Great Wall of China, which extends nearly 4,000 miles (6,437 kilometers) across northern China's rugged terrain.

chambers. The central chambers—deep pits with sloping walls—probably held the remains of kings. Thousands of sacrificial victims were buried near the entrances to the main ramps to serve the kings in the **afterlife.** The Shang also buried royalty with valuable objects made from materials such as jade, stone, shell, and bone.

Changan

Emerging in 207 B.C., the Han dynasty built great centers of trade and commerce in ancient China. The city of Changan served as the capital of this dynasty from 206 B.C. to A.D. 23. Located about 12 miles (19 km) outside the present-day city of Xian, Changan stood on a plain near the Wei River. A canal carried water from the Wei to the city.

Using the hangtu method, workers constructed a large, defensive wall around Changan. A moat dug outside the wall provided added protection from invaders and carried waste from the city to the Wei River. Inside the wall, five palaces were built in areas set aside for royalty, nobility, and administration. Each palace sat on a hangtu platform. Within each palace district were factories that made weapons to help fortify the city.

Only about 10 percent of Changan was reserved for ordinary citizens. Planners placed houses close together in rows. At its height, the city supported about 300,000 people, including some who may have lived outside the protective wall. Another section of the city

Succeeding Chinese dynasties built many structures on top of the ancient site of Changan (modern Xian). Here, experts work to restore a mosque (Islamic house of prayer) that dates to the eighth century A.D.

More than 8,000 clay warriors fill the 3-acre (1.23-hectare) vault of Qin Shihuangdi. The Han ruler ordered the building of his vast underground tomb in 247 B.C.

held the marketplace, where merchants, farmers, and craftspeople offered their wares. Roads connected all parts of the city, and a major thoroughfare that circled the inside of the city wall served as a route for patrolling soldiers.

The Han was the first dynasty to adorn Chinese cities with parks and gardens. Located outside the city wall, the parks of Changan featured ponds, streams, and elegantly landscaped hills. Exotic plants and animals thrived in these areas. Within the city wall, trees lined the roads, and private gardens grew outside the houses of the nobles.

The vast tombs of the 12 Han rulers lay outside Changan. Symbolic of the wealth of these leaders, the graves held abundant food, fine silks, musical instruments, and artifacts of bronze and jade.

Rulers were honored and protected in death as in life. In the tomb of Qin Shihuangdi, the fifth ruler of the Han dynasty, for example, archaeologists found about 8,000 clay warriors, horses, and chariots. This life-size army was meant to protect the leader during his journey into the afterlife. Each human figure bears a different face.

Early in the first century A.D., Changan was destroyed during a rebellion. The Han dynasty abandoned the city and named Lo-yang its new capital in A.D. 25.

ANCIENT CITIES OF THE MEDITERRANEAN

The first European civilizations arose along the northern shores of the Mediterranean Sea about 4,000 years ago. The sea offered access to North Africa and the Middle East, and many Europeans along the Mediterranean coast became seafaring traders. Two peoples, the Greeks and the Romans, at various times, controlled large Mediterranean empires.

Greece

Lying in the northeastern Mediterranean, Greece is made up of a mountainous mainland and hundreds of small islands. Because many regions of Greece were isolated by mountains or water, no single city or ruler was able to conquer the entire territory. As a result, ancient Greece consisted of many independent **city-states,** each of which ruled nearby villages and countryside. During the height of ancient Greece's prosperity, the city-states also conquered distant lands far beyond their seats of power.

Greece's location on a busy sea led the Greeks to become skilled sailors. Shipbuilders crafted large

An acropolis—an ancient Greek stronghold that held the main temples and most important public buildings of a city-state—still dominates the skyline of modern Athens.

Stonework was an important defensive and artistic feature of early Greek buildings. On fortifications, the stones might be thick and roughly cut (left), *while delicate carvings* (below) *might decorate the exteriors of homes and public buildings.*

fleets that traded with cities throughout the Mediterranean region. During the seventh and eighth centuries B.C., a time of widespread commercial expansion, Greek cities grew wealthy and populations increased.

Neighboring city-states often fought against one another. For this reason, builders constructed thick defensive walls, which followed an irregular path over the natural contours of the land. To make the walls, skilled masons carefully cut and fit together stones so that no cement was needed. At certain points along the walls, stone lookout towers rose to heights of three

The ruins of Delphi, an historic Greek religious site, overlook the foothills of Mount Parnassus. The main temple was dedicated to Apollo, the Greek god of music and poetry. Within this building was a chamber set aside for the Delphic Oracle—a female who interpreted messages from Apollo.

or four stories. Guarded gates with wooden doors that were locked at night provided access to the city.

Another common defensive feature of Greek city-states was a fortress called an **acropolis,** which also held buildings used for governmental and religious purposes. For easy protection, the acropolis usually sat on the city's highest point, where residents could find safety during an attack. Greek citizens also came to the acropolis to worship at temples and shrines dedicated to the Greek gods.

The most important meeting place in Greek city-states was a large area called the **agora,** or

Dominated by an acropolis, the city of Rhodes is located on the Greek island of the same name. In ancient times, the city drew its wealth from trade and was home to many writers and artists. In the A.D. 1300s, soldiers from western Europe took control of Rhodes and added more walls and towers to the hilltop fortress.

public square. The paved square was bordered by rows of columns that supported a roof. Within the agora stood buildings that housed city records, public offices, statues, and monuments. Citizens often gathered in the agora on social and religious occasions. City officials discussed new policies at the agora, which also served as a marketplace.

City-states added to their prestige by staging public entertainment and festivals. Actors, for example, put on plays about twice a year during religious festivals that honored Dionysus, the Greek god of wine. During this time, residents put aside their work, closed their shops, and crowded into the city's large, outdoor theater. Workers built the stone theaters in the shape of a semicircle. Sloped tiers of seats curved around the stage. Sometimes the seats were built into the

A drawing of the ancient marketplace in Athens shows vendors selling their wares amid a crowd of soldiers and shoppers.

sides of hills where the land below formed a natural depression for the stage.

Other spectator events took place at stadiums. A stadium was a narrow, circular track surrounded by tiered seats. Crowds cheered from the stands as athletes competed in footraces and other contests. The most famous Greek stadium was at Olympia, where the first Olympic Games were held.

The old seaport of Epidaurus is the site of one of the best-preserved Greek theaters. More than 30 rows of seats— enough to accommodate an audience of 6,000 spectators—rise steeply from the stage.

The Acropolis of Athens

One of the most powerful of the Greek city-states was Athens, the Greek world's cultural hub. In the fifth century B.C., during a wealthy period called the Golden Age, Athens reached the height of its prosperity. Famous philosophers, playwrights, architects, astronomers, and mathematicians lived and taught in this city, now the

The most important structure on the acropolis in Athens was the Parthenon (above), a temple devoted to the goddess Athena. To raise the temple's columns (left), builders layered circular drums of marble that were sized smaller near the top to give the column a tapered look.

capital of Greece. The ancient Athenians also created a democratic system of government that has influenced lawmakers for centuries.

The most famous Athenian ruins stand on the city's acropolis, a flat-topped, rocky hill that overlooks the city. The largest building on the acropolis is the Parthenon, a white marble temple that was dedicated to the city's patron goddess Athena. An enormous rectangular building supported by 46 columns,

A lioness guards her cubs in one of the marble sculptures that ornaments the buildings on the acropolis in Athens.

A view of the Erechtheum, which was built on the acropolis to honor the founders of Athens, shows the Porch of the Caryatids. These carved female figures support a roof with an overhead frieze (decorated band).

the Parthenon measures 237 feet (72 m) long, 110 feet (34 m) wide, and stands 60 feet (18 m) high. Another temple on the acropolis, the Erechtheum, is known for its south porch. Six columns called **caryatids,** sculpted to look like women, supported the temple's roof.

After entering the acropolis through a huge structure called the Propylaea, ancient Athenians passed by an elaborate gold and ivory statue of Athena. A defensive stone wall surrounded the acropolis. Wells cut into the rock tapped underground springs that supplied fresh water to the fortress during times of attack.

Roman Cities

Rome, a civilization that was centered on the Italian Peninsula west of Greece, modeled its society after

THE PALACE OF KNOSSOS

In 1900 British archaeologist Arthur Evans began excavating the ruins of Knossos, an ancient city on the island of Crete in the Aegean Sea. Knossos was the center of the Minoan culture, which flourished from about 3000 B.C. to 1450 B.C. Amid the rubble of the city's houses and administrative buildings, Evans discovered the ruins of an enormous palace.

Covering more than 5 acres (2 hectares), the ceremonial rooms, residential quarters, kitchens, workshops, and storerooms of the complex encircled a central courtyard. Inside the multistoried palace, colorful frescoes (paintings made on wet plaster) decorated the corridors. Excavators also discovered an elaborate plumbing system.

Evans went beyond excavation in his study of the palace. He reconstructed much of the complex, replacing rotted wooden columns with concrete pillars painted the original shade of deep red. Workers reinforced staircases and walls with steel girders, concrete, and new stone. In addition, Evans restored the crumbling frescoes. Although some archaeologists question the accuracy of the reconstructed palace, many more experts believe his efforts have brought Minoan history to life.

The restored Palace of Knossos on the island of Crete features painted columns and colorful wall paintings.

those of the Greeks and the Etruscans. These two previous cultures had built settlements on the peninsula. From the Greeks, the Romans adopted some artistic, cultural, and scientific principles. Among the many techniques that Roman architects learned from Etruscan builders was the way to fashion round structures of brick or stone.

But the Romans did not just imitate earlier building styles. They also broadened the scope of previous Greek and Etruscan architectural ideas. Unlike the Greeks, who carefully chiseled and fit together each stone of their buildings, the Romans used bricks and mortar. These materials were abundant, lighter, easier to handle, and could

The ancient Romans were innovators in design and construction. This stone sculpture depicts workers powering a crane that lifts artisans to the roof.

Early Roman builders excelled in the use of clay bricks to make supporting arches. The raw materials for the bricks—clay and water, as well as abundant sunshine for drying—were plentiful on the Italian Peninsula, the homeland of the Romans.

be produced in large quantities. Although the Romans made most of their structures out of brick, they still appreciated the beauty of stone. For this reason, Roman workers often covered brick walls with smooth slabs of marble.

The Romans also invented many new construction techniques. For example, vaults (arched ceilings) made it possible to roof a large building without filling the inside space with support columns. Using their engineering and design skills,

In the center of Rome, the capital of the Roman Empire, stands the Pantheon, one of the world's most complete ancient temples. Completed in about A.D. 126, the circular structure was made of concrete and brick and had a spacious, well-lit interior. The Romans were the first builders to use concrete—a mixture of sand, gravel, and water—as a construction material.

the Romans put up huge stadiums, marketplaces, aqueducts, and even apartment buildings, some of which were as much as five stories high.

Planning the Colonies

The ancient Romans were seafarers, traders, and warriors who sailed large ships across the Mediterranean. To increase their wealth and power, the Romans began to invade neighboring lands. By the first century A.D., the Romans controlled an enormous empire and had established many colonies in other lands. Most Roman colonial cities had one of two purposes. The city was either a military base set up to protect conquered territories, or it was a strategically located seaport designed to improve trade.

As their empire expanded and as colonies were quickly founded, the

Built in Rome in A.D. 113, Trajan's Column commemorates the emperor Trajan's defeat of the Dacians, a people of central Europe. Carvings of events in the Dacian wars climb up the 100-foot (30-meter) pillar.

Romans devised a standard plan for their cities. Square or rectangular in shape, each city had two main roads—one running east to west and another going north to south. The place where these two roads met was the center of town. All other streets ran parallel to the two main roads. These streets intersected at right angles to form city blocks that the Romans called islands. The city was enclosed by a strong wall, and the two main roads passed through four gates, one on each wall.

The founding of a new Roman city involved many religious rituals. The Romans believed, for example, that by plowing a single row where a city's wall was to be built, the Roman gods would know which borders to defend. The settlers then carefully built the entire city within these borders.

On the highest point of every Roman city, workers constructed a temple to honor the Roman gods Jupiter, Juno, and Minerva. In his writings, the ancient Roman architect Vitruvius described the perfect locations for shrines and temples. According to Vitruvius, a temple in honor of Mercury, the god of trade and travel, should dominate the **forum**—a Roman civic center. Shrines in honor of Isis and Serapis, the gods of fertility and of the underworld, were put in the business quarter. Next to the city's theater, stood a shrine dedicated either to Apollo, the god of the sun, or to Bacchus, the god of wine.

Roman warships patrolled the Mediterranean Sea to protect Roman merchant fleets. The Romans, who had created a vast empire by A.D. 100, built many port cities in their conquered territories and established extensive trading networks.

Roman city planners followed in the wake of the Roman army as it conquered parts of Europe, the Middle East, and North Africa. This aerial view of the Roman ruins of Timgad, a site now in the North African country of Algeria, shows the city's gridlike street design. Roman architects in Timgad built a theater, a forum (civic center), and several bathhouses.

Public Buildings

The technical skills and engineering abilities of the Romans provided some conveniences that few other ancient communities enjoyed. City streets were wide, straight, and paved. Aqueducts brought clean

A sturdy Roman wall still stands in the English countryside, nearly 2,000 years after its construction.

Visitors inspect the ruins of the Colosseum (left) in Rome. Tiered seats rose from the arena's floor, which consisted of tight-fitting wooden planks covered with a layer of sand. The rows closest to the floor were for the most influential Romans, while the topmost seating, or gallery, was for ordinary spectators. A triumphal arch (below) honors the Roman emperor Lucius Septimius Severus, a skilled military commander who ruled in the second century A.D.

The forum of Rome was the city's main public gathering area. One section housed crowded markets, and another was set aside for public speeches. Courts of law, as well as the Roman Senate, occupied opposite sides of the main square.

water from the countryside to the city, and elaborate sewage systems removed waste efficiently.

Roman cities also provided residents with a rich and exciting cultural life. Accomplished actors staged plays that drew crowds to the urban theaters. Most communities had a large, open-air building called an **amphitheater** for athletic games, and a stadium called a **hippodrome** for horse races. Rome's Colosseum, the largest of all the ancient amphitheaters, held 45,000 people and was built with an intricate network of stables, passageways, dressing rooms, and storerooms. After 2,000 years, the Colosseum is still largely intact in the modern city of Rome.

Ancient Roman life centered around the public forum, a roofless area surrounded by a series of arches and columns. Next to the forum stood an enclosed building called a **basilica,** which served as

a marketplace during the cold and rainy winter months.

Also close to the forum was the public bathhouse, one of the most distinctive features of the Roman lifestyle. The bathhouse was divided into separate sections for men and women. Each section was further divided into various rooms, which had pools of either cold, lukewarm, or hot water. Bathhouses in the larger cities also had rooms where visitors could get a massage, exercise, or chat with other bathers.

Roman architects used their skills not only for the construction of theaters, aqueducts, and bridges but also for monuments. Triumphal arches were put up to honor emperors and other important people or to commemorate events, such as military victories. Many of these tall triumphal arches are still standing today, adorned with elaborate sculptures and inscriptions explaining the purpose of the monuments.

The Ruins of Pompeii

During the first century A.D., the Roman city of Pompeii in southwestern Italy was a busy trading port and industrial center. Pompeii's warm climate and beautiful scenery attracted many wealthy Romans, who built elaborate villas along the Mediterranean coast. This prosperity ended during the summer of A.D. 79, however, when the nearby volcano Mount Vesuvius erupted, burying the city in a thick layer of ash.

The volcanic ash preserved the city until it was discovered in the 1700s. Since that time, archaeologists have excavated about three-fourths of the ancient city. Pompeii was laid out in an oval shape and was surrounded by a thick defensive wall with seven gates. The city's streets crossed at right angles and were paved with blocks of hardened lava, which had formed after earlier eruptions of Mount Vesuvius. The volcanic ash preserved the streets so well that wheel ruts can still be seen in the pavement. In the center of Pompeii was a forum surrounded by other important public buildings. The city also had a theater, an amphithe-

The residents of Pompeii, a busy southwestern seaport on the Italian Peninsula, cower as nearby Mount Vesuvius erupts in A.D. 79. The volcano buried the city in a thick layer of ash, which preserved the ruins for more than 1,500 years.

Excavators have unearthed much of Pompeii, whose wide streets and well-built temples, marketplaces, and dwellings attracted a population of about 20,000 people.

ater, several temples, and three public baths.

Experts have restored many of Pompeii's houses and public buildings. Visitors can now wander through most sections of the city and see how the ancient Romans lived. Large estates included stables, barns, orchards, and gardens. Dwellings often had rooms grouped around a central reception area. On main streets, merchants lived in chambers above or behind their shops. Each small section of Pompeii that archaeologists uncover reveals additional details about Roman city planning and the everyday lives of the ancient Romans.

ANCIENT CITIES OF THE AMERICAS

Archaeologists and other experts are still piecing together much of the early history of the Americas. For many decades, scholars have studied the remains of buildings, temples, pottery, and sculptures in Mexico, Guatemala, Belize, El Salvador, Honduras, Peru, and Bolivia. From these studies, archaeologists have learned how ancient people in this area lived, worked, and worshiped.

The Olmec and the Maya

The region called Mesoamerica includes the modern nations of Mexico, Honduras, Guatemala, Belize, and El Salvador, where the remains of several ancient cultures have long fascinated archaeologists. One of the oldest groups known to have inhabited Mesoamerica is the Olmec, who lived in the wet lowlands along Mexico's southeastern coast beginning in about 1200 B.C.

Evidence of this still-mysterious culture lies mainly in Olmec sculptures, which range from huge stone heads to delicately carved jade figurines. Archaeologists have also studied the remains of squat, clay pyramids, ceremonial plazas, and jade-filled tombs built by the Olmec. Although these important finds have provided some clues to Olmec life, scientists have not yet discovered the remains of an early city.

The largest ancient sculptures in the Americas were crafted by Olmec artisans, whose culture flourished beginning in about 1200 B.C. Carved of basalt, a dark gray rock, this huge head was found in La Venta, a village in southeastern Mexico.

This baffling civilization, whose sculptures have been found throughout Mesoamerica, was imitated by succeeding cultures. Olmec artistic and architectural styles—as well as reverence for the jaguar, a favorite Olmec figure—turned up in the ancient Mayan civilization that populated what are now Guatemala, Honduras, Belize, and southeastern Mexico.

The Mayan civilization, which flourished from the third to the ninth centuries A.D., was centered in the tropical rain forests of northern Guatemala. Here, archaeologists discovered the ruins of Tikal and Uaxactún. Other major Mayan ruins exist at Copán in Honduras and at Uxmal, Chichén-Itzá, and Palenque in Mexico.

From the remains of Mayan buildings, archaeologists know that the Maya were great architects with a sophisticated understanding of mathematics and astronomy. They had perfected a system of hieroglyphics that has helped modern

The Mayan ruins of Uxmal in southeastern Mexico include a ceremonial ball court and a pyramid-shaped temple. The Maya, who lived in many parts of Mesoamerica—a region that includes Mexico and much of Central America— thrived from the third to the ninth centuries A.D.

In the sixth century B.C., a Mayan artist decorated this ceremonial jar with sculpted heads and picture symbols.

scholars begin to put together the puzzle of ancient Mayan history.

Some scholars suggest that places like Tikal and Copán were not permanently inhabited cities but rather religious and governmental centers serving the surrounding lands. People from the countryside may have gathered at these sites for a short period and then returned to their permanent homes in the outlying rural area. Excavations of houses and other buildings that fan out from these centers support this conclusion.

A deeply religious people, the Maya worshiped many gods, whose help and blessing were sought through festivals and sacrifices performed by priests. Tikal and Copán

Mayan priests climbed a steep flight of steps to reach the altar of a temple (left) at Tikal in northern Guatemala. At Palenque, a city in southeastern Mexico, workers built the royal palace (below) of stone and then covered the surface with plaster.

both have tall limestone pyramids with long, steep flights of stairs. On top of the pyramids stood small temples, where religious ceremonies were conducted. Priests climbed the stairs to reach the temple altars and to celebrate rituals that welcomed the New Year or asked for a good harvest.

In addition to tall pyramids, Mayan cities had long, low buildings, where priests and government leaders may have lived during festivals. To connect buildings, the Maya constructed archways, whose inside walls gradually sloped until only a small gap remained at the top. Builders then sealed the gap with rows of flat stones. Archae-ologists have also uncovered tall **stelae,** on which Mayan hieroglyphics record dates and important political events. By deciphering the picture writing, scholars have learned much about Mayan history.

The Grandeur of Teotihuacán

West of the Mayan lands, near what is now Mexico City, flourished an unnamed group that borrowed Olmec styles. Although archaeologists have yet to identify the culture, they do know the name of the group's capital city—Teotihuacán. This name, given by later inhabitants of Mexico called the

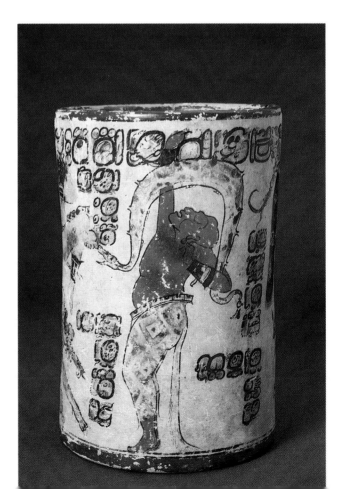

The Maya, who handcrafted their simple jars, dishes, and other vessels, were accomplished potters who traded common household wares, as well as decorative pots (right).

Aztecs, means "city of the gods." According to many experts, this site is the first true urban center of the Americas.

Covering an area of about 8 square miles (21 sq km), Teotihuacán consists of a vast planned city dominated by two huge structures—the Pyramid of the Moon and the Pyramid of the Sun. From studying pieces of pottery and charcoal, materials that can be scientifically dated, archaeologists believe the site was originally inhabited in the first century A.D. About 400 years later, at the height of the city's prestige, a population of approximately 125,000 people, including farmers, artisans, traders, merchants, and priests, lived in Teotihuacán.

Like Mayan centers, Teotihuacán had a religious focus. At the north end of the city was the Pyramid of

The Pyramid of the Sun at Teotihuacán dwarfs visitors to the ancient site near Mexico City. At its height, in about the fifth century A.D., Teotihuacán governed a large territory in central Mexico and had a population of as many as 125,000 people.

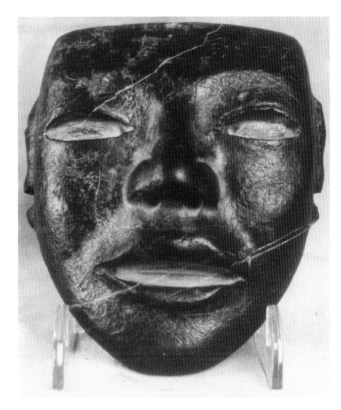

An artisan from Teotihuacán crafted this death mask of black stone in about A.D. 700, not long before the city was abandoned.

the Moon, a stone, earth, and adobe (sun-baked clay) structure with a base that measured 400 square feet (37 sq m). Extending from the Pyramid of the Moon was a long, straight boulevard, which the Aztecs called the Avenue of the Dead. Near the middle of the 2-mile (3-km) avenue was the Pyramid of the Sun. From a base of 700 square feet (65 sq m) rose a broad, steep stairway topped by an altar. At the end of the avenue was a complex that included the Temple of Quetzlcóatl, a shrine to one of the gods revered by the city's inhabitants.

Set in a strict grid plan, the city spread out in every direction. Houses, marketplaces, and shops were designed to be pleasant, spacious, and practical. Dwellings in each of the one-story, concrete apartment houses opened onto a patio. Colorful and detailed murals decorated many of the walls in these houses. Excavations of marketplaces have revealed deep holes for the support posts of canopied stalls, where the carved artworks of the city's craftspeople were bought and sold.

In about 750, Teotihuacán was destroyed. Because no foreign weapons have been uncovered on the site, archaeologists believe the city's fall was the work of an internal uprising.

The modern Mexican muralist Diego Rivera painted this image of the bustling Aztec marketplace at Tlatelolco, which was linked by a causeway (a raised earthen road) to the capital of Tenochtitlán. The city's Great Temple is in the background on the right.

The Aztecs

The eventual successors to Mexico City and the surrounding area were the Aztecs. Beginning in the thirteenth century, this group allied with and then conquered the surrounding peoples, founding a large empire. For funds to run the empire, Aztec leaders taxed the con-

quered territories. As part of their religious rituals, the Aztecs sacrificed prisoners.

Because Aztec planners admired the layout of the ruined city of Teotihuacán, they designed the Aztec capital city of Tenochtitlán on a similarly vast scale. Founded in about 1325, the chosen site was a small island in a lake. Engineers built canals for transportation within the city and constructed causeways (raised earthen roads) to connect Tenochtitlán to the mainland.

Tenochtitlán consisted of four major districts, each divided into smaller plots of land. The main quadrant of the city held the Great Temple, an imposing pyramid where human sacrifices and other important Aztec rituals took place. The palace of the Aztec leader, which doubled as the hub of administration, also stood in this area.

In 1521 Spanish explorers eliminated the Aztec culture by taking over Tenochtitlán and by defeating the Aztec ruler. The Spaniards leveled the city and built Mexico City in its place. Because of this destruction, very little original Aztec architecture remains.

Throughout the twentieth century, archaeologists have worked hard to piece together the story of Tenochtitlán's Great Temple. Their studies, as well as a careful examination of Spanish diaries of the 1500s, have revealed that the temple stood in its own rectangular zone or precinct, which was surrounded by a stone wall. Within the wall stood a smaller temple to Quetzlcóatl and a ceremonial ball court in which a game similar to basketball was played.

On the altar of the Great Temple in Tenochtitlán, Aztec priests sacrificed humans to the Aztec gods during religious ceremonies.

Resembling the ruins at Tikal and Teotihuacán, the Great Temple was a pyramid, which rose in several tiers. Two steep stairways led to a platform on which sat two structures—a shrine to the rain god Tlaloc and a shrine to Huitzilopochtli, the god of war. In front of the shrines were broad stone blocks on which captive peoples were stretched for sacrifice.

Excavation of the site, which took place in the late 1970s and early 1980s, was complicated by centuries of urban development. Workers uncovered numerous artifacts, including offering urns, religious statues, ceremonial knives, and a dedication stone. From these items as well as from hieroglyphics, crews identified seven main periods of construction, during which time the complex was enlarged by the addition of platforms and smaller temples. Destroyed by the Spaniards in 1521, little is left of the latest temple complex, but remains from the earlier building periods are extensive and are still being studied by archaeologists.

The Incas

Archaeologists probably know less about ruins in South America than they do about sites in Mesoamerica. Yet there is tantalizing evidence of several ancient cultures, most of which thrived along the coasts.

In southern Peru, people made their homes in adobe buildings and buried their dead in woven garments. Some newly discovered remains of the Moche people, dating

A model of Tenochtitlán shows the city's main quarter, which held the Great Temple (center) as well as other religious and governmental buildings.

Weavers from the Nazca culture, which thrived in southern Peru from about 200 B.C. to A.D. 600, produced this burial cloth covered with figures dressed in colorful ceremonial robes.

from around A.D. 100, are only now being excavated and examined in northern Peru. Chan Chan, a planned community of the Chimu kingdom, was established in northern Peru during the thirteenth century A.D. Evidence of Chan Chan came to light after heavy rains washed away centuries of soil and revealed the city's earthen remains.

In the fifteenth century, Chimu and other regional realms fell to the Incas, a powerful highland group that crossed the Andes Mountains to reach the coast. By the late 1400s, the Incas controlled a vast empire along the Pacific shores of South America. But like the Aztec Empire, the Incan civilization was destroyed by Spanish explorers, who conquered and looted the Incan capital of Cuzco in 1532.

Sitting 11,000 feet (3,353 m) above sea level, Cuzco was the heart of the Incan Empire. At the outskirts of the city stood many single-story thatched houses made of adobe on a stone foundation. More adobe homes stretched along narrow, paved, gridlike streets. Down the middle of these roads, stone-lined channels carried running water, which took household wastes out of the city.

In the center of Cuzco were two large squares, one for festivals and

The ruins of Chan Chan (above), the capital of the Chimu kingdom, lie along the northwestern coast of Peru. Heavy rains that fell in the early twentieth century damaged the city, whose buildings were made of mud. Tourists study a mural (left) depicting the city of Cuzco, Peru, as it would have looked in the 1400s when the city served as the capital of the Incan Empire.

the other for the palaces of Incan leaders. South of these squares was Coricancha, also known as the Temple of the Sun, whose stonework amazed the Europeans. In fact, masonry was perhaps the most highly developed skill of Incan builders. Incan masons fitted heavy stones—without the use of mortar—to heights of several stories.

After the initial Spanish takeover of Cuzco, the Incas fought back and in the process set fire to the city. On the charred ruins, the Spaniards built cathedrals, churches, public buildings, and other structures. Although they conquered the Incan capital, the Spanish invaders never found Machu Picchu, a hard-to-reach Incan religious site in the Andes Mountains. Machu Picchu remained untouched until 1911, when the U.S. explorer Hiram Bingham came upon what was then called "the lost city of the Incas."

Probably too small to be considered a city, Machu Picchu consisted of 200 structures and is likely to have housed a permanent, self-sustaining population of about 1,000 people. The existence of houses and other buildings suggests a well-ordered community, in which each district had its own function. An industrial district, for example, may have housed masons, artisans, and other craftspeople. A farming community probably worked terraced farmland and stored the harvest in granaries.

The large number of Incan religious structures at Machu Picchu helped archaeologists conclude that this spot was sacred to the Incas. Incan builders constructed the sanctuary in the mid-1400s high in the Andes Mountains of Peru.

73

The large number of religious buildings at Machu Picchu has led most archaeologists to consider it a sacred place. Experts have examined three major ritual sites—the Temple of the Sun, the Temple of Three Windows, and the Principal Temple—as well as mausoleums (above-ground tombs). Perhaps the holiest place in Machu Picchu was an altar called *inti-huatana,* where Incan priests and astronomers observed the sky and worshiped the sun. Although archaeologists are still trying to explain the mysteries of Machu Picchu, it is clear the site had great spiritual meaning for the Incas.

Cities of the Future

As the world continues to change, so will the ways in which cities are built. More than 2.4 billion people—43 percent of the world's total population—now live in urban areas. Experts predict that by the beginning of the twenty-first century about 5 million more people will have moved to already crowded cities. For this reason, city planners will have to work to accommodate increasing populations in existing urban areas, as well as to design new cities that offer sufficient housing and jobs.

During the 1900s, suburbs arose outside many cities. People who live in these secondary urban communities often work in the central city, but businesses are increasingly expanding into the suburbs, too. Many experts believe that eventually the suburbs and cities will run together into a continuous metropolitan area called a **megalopolis.** In the United States, for example, the area between Washington, D.C., and Boston, Massachusetts, is quickly becoming such a megalopolis.

Besides overcrowding, cities also face traffic and pollution problems. In Rome, for instance, car exhaust and the continuous rumbling of large vehicles has caused the Colosseum to corrode and crumble. To ease traffic congestion, many governments may begin building more mass transit systems, constructing special roads for different kinds of vehicles, or even making electronic highways where individual cars can be programmed for certain destinations. To improve air quality, cities may someday be enclosed within temperature-controlled plastic domes equipped with electronic air filters.

The development and improvement of cities is a slow process. As in ancient times, city planners must carefully examine the urban environment and figure out how their designs can improve the lives of city dwellers. By studying ancient cities, planners can learn from the successes and failures of the first builders.

Wide avenues lined by modern skyscrapers cut through São Paulo, the largest city and main industrial hub of Brazil. The city holds many universities, museums, and public parks, as well as factories that produce a wide variety of goods. Suburbs fan out from the center of São Paulo, whose metropolitan population reached more than 12 million in the mid-1990s.

PRONUNCIATION GUIDE

A surveyor maps the site of an ancient city.

Akhenaton (ahkeh-NAHT-uhn)

caryatid (KAHR-ee-aht-ihd)

Chichén-Itzá
  (chih-chehn—iht-SAH)

Euphrates (yoo-FRAYT-eez)

Giza (GEE-zuh)

hangtu (HAHNG-TOO)

hieroglyphic (hy-ihr-oh-GLIF-ik)

Huitzilopochtli
  (hwee-TZIHL-oh-pok-tlee)

inti-huatana
  (ihn-tee—HWAH-tah-nah)

Machu Picchu mahtchoo
  PEEK-tchoo

megalopolis
  (mehg-uh-LAAP-uh-less)

Mesopotamia
  (mehs-uh-puh-TAY-mee-uh)

Moche (MOH-chay)

Mohenjo-Daro
  (moh-hehn-joh—DAHR-oh)

Nebuchadnezzar
  (nehb-yuh-kuhd-NEHZ-uhr)

Palenque (puh-LENG-kay)

pharaoh (fehr-OH)

Pompeii (pahm-PAY)

Propylaea (proh-puh-LEE-uh)

Qin Shihuangdi (CHIHN
  SHIH-WAHNG-DEE)

Quetzalcoátl
  (keht-SAHL-kwoht-uhl)

Tenochtitlán
  (tay-notch-tee-TLAHN)

Teotihuacán (tay-oh-tee
  wuh-KAHN)

Tlaloc (TLUH-lohk)

Uaxactún (wash-ahk-TOON)

Uxmal (ooz-MAHL)

Vesuvius (vuh-SOO-vee-uhs)

Xian (SHEE-AHN)

Zhengzhou (JUNG-JOH)

ziggurat (ZIHG-uh-raht)

GLOSSARY

acropolis: a stronghold in an ancient Greek city that was built at the city's highest point and contained its chief temples and public buildings.

afterlife: an existence after death.

agora: an open space in an ancient Greek city that was used as a marketplace or a general meeting place.

amphitheater: an open, circular space surrounded by rising tiers of seats. Amphitheaters were the sites of spectator sports in ancient Greece.

aqueduct: an artificial channel for carrying water. Most aqueducts are raised brick structures supported by arches.

archaeologist: a scientist who studies the material remains of past human life.

basilica: a large meeting hall in an ancient Roman city in which public officials conducted day-to-day business.

caryatid: a sculpted female figure used as a column to support a roof.

city-state: a self-ruling state in ancient Greece that consisted of a city and the territory that surrounded it.

excavate: to dig out and remove objects from an archaeological site.

forum: the public square of an ancient Roman city.

hieroglyphic: a system of writing that uses picture-characters. Both the Egyptian and the Mayan civilizations wrote with hieroglyphics.

hippodrome: an oval arena for horse races and chariot races in ancient Greece or Rome.

megalopolis: a thickly populated area that consists of one or more large cities and many smaller, surrounding cities.

moat: a deep, wide trench, usually filled with water, that was built outside a fortified wall for defensive purposes.

pictograph: an ancient drawing that stood for a word or a sound. Pictographs were a step in the invention of writing.

public works: structures, such as schools, highways, and docks, built for public use with public money.

rampart: a stone or earthen wall surrounding a fortified city for defensive purposes.

stela: a carved stone slab or pillar whose markings commemorate a person or a special event.

ziggurat: a rectangular temple-tower rising from a wide base to smaller, higher stages. Each successive stage was reached by a ramp.

INDEX

A stone carving from Nimrud in Iraq shows soldiers battling invaders from atop the ancient city's protective wall.

Many ancient city dwellers decorated the floors of their homes with colorful mosaics—pictures made with small pieces of colored material held together with cement.

Photo Acknowledgments

Bob Zehring, pp. 2, 45 (bottom), 49, 52, 56 (top); Minneapolis Public Library and Information Center, pp. 7, 57; Tennessee State Museum, from a painting by Carlyle Urello, p. 8; Independent Picture Service, pp. 9, 11, 16, 18 (bottom), 27, 30, 31, 34, 43, 46 (top and bottom), 47, 50, 51, 54, 55 (top), 63, 78, 79; Israel Government Tourist Office, p. 10; The Mansell Collection, pp. 12, 58; Dr. Steven Derfler, pp. 13 (top and bottom), 76; Staatliche Museen, Berlin / Bildarchiv Preussischer Kulturbesitz, p. 15; Jerusalem Publishing House, p. 17; University of Minnesota, College of Architecture and Landscape Architecture, pp. 18 (top), 19, 20, 22; Drs. A. A. M. van der Heyden, Naarden, the Netherlands, pp. 21, 23 (bottom), 24, 41, 56 (bottom), 61; Mary Ellen Sigmond, pp. 23 (top), 42 (top and bottom); John H. Peck, p. 25; by Charles Chipiez, courtesy University of Minnesota College of Architecture and Landscape Architecture, p. 26; Archaeological Survey of India, courtesy University of Minnesota College of Architecture and Lanscape Architecture, p. 29 (top); Embassy of Pakistan, p. 29 (bottom); Bill Kish, p. 32; Pakistan Tourism Development Corporation, p. 33; Nelson-Atkins Museum of Art, pp. 35 (top and bottom), 67; Smithsonian Institution, p. 36; Steve Feinstein, p. 37; M. Eugene Gilliom, p. 38; William Thompson, p. 39; Meredith Pillon / Greek National Tourist Organization, p. 44; The Bettmann Archive, p. 45 (top); Daniel H. Condit, pp. 48, 53, 59; Kenneth C. Poertner, pp. 62, 64 (top and bottom), 70, 72 (bottom), 73; Stuart Rome, p. 65; Mexican Government Tourist Authority, pp. 66, 68; Library of Congress, p. 69; Museum of Fine Arts, Boston, p. 71; Tom Trow, p. 72 (top); VARIG Airlines, p. 75.

Cover photographs: Drs. A. A. M. van der Heyden, Naarden, the Netherlands (front) and Dr. Steven Derfler (back).